M000046318

F*CK
worry

F*CK WORRY

An Hachette UK Company
www.hachette.co.uk

Vie Books, an imprint of Summersdale Publishers Ltd
Part of Octopus Publishing Group Limited
Carmelite House
50 Victoria Embankment
LONDON
EC4Y 0DZ
UK

www.summersdale.com

Printed and bound in China

ISBN: 978-1-78783-010-3

Substantial discounts on bulk quantities of Summersdale books are available to corporations, professional associations and other organizations. For details contact general enquiries: telephone: +44 (0) 1243 771107 or email: enquiries@summersdale.com.

F*CK

worry

*Tips and Advice on
How to Overcome Your* Fears

ALEX MARTIN

INTRODUCTION

Worrying is a part of life – if human beings didn't worry about things, we wouldn't be the world-conquering, wheel-inventing superspecies that we are. In short, without our ancestors worrying about the sabre-tooth tiger that might be lurking outside their cave, we wouldn't be here – most of our gene pools would have been abruptly ended by the aforementioned sabre-tooth tigers several millennia ago.

While life-threatening danger is not quite so common today, our brains haven't quite got the memo, and we get the same "fight, flight or freeze" feelings when we perceive potential threats to our well-being. Worrying about important events or people we love is perfectly normal and helps us to prepare for the unknown and find solutions to problems.

But sustained worrying or anxiety harms your mental and physical health, as well as affecting your relationships, sleep patterns and central nervous system.

While this book can't eliminate worry completely from your life, handling anxiety becomes much easier when you have some tried and tested strategies to calm an anxious mind and build a more resilient mental outlook.

So, whether you're a constant worrier or a 3 a.m. stress-head, read on. Take what works for you and let go of what doesn't.

ANXIETY'S LIKE A ROCKING CHAIR. IT GIVES YOU SOMETHING TO DO, BUT IT DOESN'T GET YOU VERY FAR.

JODI PICOULT

F*CK EXPECTATIONS

Come to everything with an open mind. It's hard not to build some things up in your mind to be a bigger deal than they are, but you simply don't know what will happen, and that's OK. So, go ahead: picture that worst-case scenario, then recognize it as just a thought (and probably an unlikely one at that), and let it go.

Try writing down what you expect to happen – seeing it in black and white can help you realize how likely or unlikely it is. Then, write down how you would like things to unfold – focus on this version but be open to curve balls.

If you're receptive to life surprising you, you'll get better and better at rolling with the punches.

YOU
ARE A
BADASS.

WHEN SH*T BRINGS YOU
DOWN, JUST SAY "F*CK IT",
AND EAT YOURSELF SOME
MOTHERF*CKING CANDY.

DAVID SEDARIS

Be real

Be yourself, do your best and let go of the idea that you can control how you're received by others. If you try to change or edit yourself to fit how you think others want you to be, you'll make yourself miserable with constant pretending. Not everyone is going to appreciate the real you, but do you know what? The people who don't appreciate you aren't your people. Be proud and unapologetic with your weirdness, your inconsistencies and your true opinions – if you don't let the real you show, how will those who are going to love you fiercely ever find you?

Take a

DEEP

f*cking breath.

Get grateful

Next time you find yourself stuck in a pattern of anxious thoughts, try this trick! Quick: name three things you're grateful for. It can be anything – a person, a place, a coincidence, the existence of hummus and tortilla chips... whatever you appreciate in the world right at this second.

This exercise forces your mind into the present moment and slams the brakes on a negative thought spiral. Getting in the habit of feeling and expressing gratitude trains your mind to focus on the positive and transforms the way you experience the world. Things you never noticed before will bring you a new joy and appreciation for the world's small pleasures.

IT'S OK TO BE SCARED. BEING SCARED MEANS YOU'RE ABOUT TO DO SOMETHING REALLY, REALLY BRAVE.

MANDY HALE

F*CKING LOVE YOURSELF

This is the secret to a calm and happy life. When you love, accept and trust yourself, you can let go of the anxious need to control what is external to you and therefore out of your control. You'll know – and truly believe – that as long as you have yourself, you will be OK.

Find little ways to show yourself love every day:

- Indulge in something that brings you pleasure like reading a good book, taking the scenic route to work or drawing.
- Speak to yourself with kindness, positivity and patience.
- Choose a prompt and each time you see it, silently say to yourself: I love you. It could be anything – from seeing red traffic lights to a bird in the sky.

Once you start treating yourself with love and gentleness, your reserves of self-love will grow and grow.

EVERYTHING'S

GOING TO BE OK.

F*CK APOLOGIZING

Swap "I'm sorry" for "thank you". Instead of "Sorry for bothering you" try "thank you for listening" ... it's so much more positive. Only apologize when you have something to apologize for. If and when you do f*ck up, apologize sincerely and make amends.

You might wonder how cutting down on your "sorrys" can help, but try looking at it this way: when you say "sorry" you're drawing attention to a perceived failing in yourself. When you say "thank you" you're showing appreciation for the kindness or generosity the other person has shown you.

SHOW UP IN EVERY
SINGLE MOMENT
LIKE YOU'RE MEANT
TO BE THERE.

MARIE FORLEO

Be more cat

Cats don't give a sh*t. For an example of a lifestyle free from stress and worry, look no further than cats.

Taking frequent naps, dedicating time to personal hygiene and maintaining cast-iron boundaries are admirable cat traits that we can all use more of in our lives.

Beyond emulating these feline Zen masters, we can watch cute YouTube cat videos, which studies have found have a significant positive effect on mood. If you or a loved one own a pet, cuddle up with a furry friend as stroking a pet reduces anxiety levels and heightens feelings of belonging and well-being. In fact, invest time in all aspects of caring for your pet because taking care of a pet serves as a brilliant confidence-booster and distraction from an anxious mind.

F*CK COMPARISONS

A lot of worry comes from looking at others' lives and feeling like we are failing in comparison. Stop. Know that 99 per cent of the time, you are only seeing what others choose to show you. You have no idea of the hurdles or helping hands that have brought them to where they are and making assumptions from an incomplete story means you're probably getting it wrong.

Everyone's path is different, and you're not in competition with anyone but your past self. Keep going, you're doing great.

YOU ARE

the sky.

EVERYTHING

else – it's just the

WEATHER.

PEMA CHÖDRÖN

FOCUS

Picturing all the things you need to do and their various deadlines can get overwhelming and distracting. So, take control of your mind and don't let it wander from the task in front of you. Know that there are only ever a maximum of two things to be done at any moment: breathe, and the task at hand.

Right now, you're reading this book, you're breathing – tick and tick. If you want to take a break from reading, that's cool. For a while, perhaps breathing's the only thing on your to-do list.

Try to remember this mindful to-do list next time you feel stressed or overwhelmed, it'll bring you back down to earth.

Worrying is

WASTED ENERGY.

Cut yourself some f*cking slack

Stop being so hard on yourself. Listen to your inner voice and consider whether you would speak to a friend like that. If not, then make some changes. You're in control and you can choose a new inner voice. Speak to yourself like you would your most precious, cherished, sensitive friend. You deserve to give yourself the same compassion you show to others.

In three words I can sum up everything I've learned about life: it goes on.

ROBERT FROST

F*CK
PERFECTION

Perfection is neither attainable nor desirable. The most accomplished, interesting, magnetic people are that way because they have embraced their imperfections, learned from failure and not let their flaws stop them from living their best life.

If you catch yourself striving for perfection and holding yourself back because of it, give yourself a break. Remind yourself that you are human and that your best is enough.

YOU ARE

MORE POWERFUL
THAN YOU THINK.

TAKE A BREAK

No task is so urgent or important that you can't take a break. When you're anxious to get something over with, it sometimes feels easier to push on through even if you're getting overwhelmed. You can always take time away from whatever you're doing or thinking. Give yourself 10 seconds, 10 minutes, 10 days to reset. The world will not end.

Try writing down all the things spinning around in your mind, no matter how silly they look on paper. That way, you can safely forget about them for as long as you need to rest and recharge.

AS SOON AS YOU
TRUST YOURSELF,
YOU WILL KNOW
HOW TO LIVE.

JOHANN WOLFGANG
VON GOETHE

LISTEN TO YOUR GUT

It can sometimes be difficult to differentiate between anxiety and intuition – both give a feeling of "knowing" something without proof. Anxiety is frantic, intuition is calm. Anxiety breaks into your thoughts, intuition comes when your mind is still. Anxiety tells a lot of stories, intuition is simple.

Try asking your intuition for guidance on small, inconsequential decisions first: almond croissant or plain? Jeans or sweatpants? Music or a podcast?

Don't overthink it, just tune in to that wise, quiet voice inside you and make a choice. Making decisions based on intuition isn't as irrational as it sounds. Studies have found that intuition is based on your brain processing information that has not yet made it to your conscious awareness, in order to keep you safe. Once you start listening to and trusting your gut feeling, you'll be able to sense it more and more clearly.

CALM

YOUR
TITS.

Move your body

Regular exercise won't just improve your physical fitness, it will work wonders on your mental health too. Physical activity increases your production of feel-good serotonin and lowers levels of feel-bad cortisol. If you attend a club or group exercise session then you can also benefit socially – the social side of exercise enhances your sense of belonging and lowers anxiety in the moment.

The key is to find a form of exercise that you enjoy. If doing something feels like a treat rather than a chore, you're more likely to form a habit and stick to it. So, take a look at what's going on near where you live and try out a few different things. Remember, exercise doesn't have to take the form of "normal" activity. You could join a climbing club, partake in some Nordic walking or learn to salsa – and much more. See what works for you and commit to a regular schedule.

TO BE A SENSITIVE
PERSON THAT
CARES A LOT, THAT
TAKES THINGS IN
IN A DEEP WAY, IS
ACTUALLY PART
OF WHAT MAKES
YOU AMAZING.

EMMA STONE

F*CK NEGATIVITY

Our surroundings affect our mindset. Remove negative influences, people and ideas from your attention and you'll find that negative thoughts are easier to control.

Unfollow any social media account that brings up feelings of inadequacy, guilt or anxiety in you. Don't waste time finishing books you're not enjoying. Listen exclusively to music that makes you want to sing along or dance around the kitchen. Fill your environment with beauty, lightness and joy and you'll start to feel the effect on your outlook.

You have

EVERYTHING

you need.

UNLEARN YOUR DEFENCE MECHANISMS

When you're growing up, your brain is constantly adapting to better protect you emotionally and physically. Worrying is one of the ways our childhood minds learned how to prepare emotionally for harm and disappointment. Anxiety feels f*cking awful, but it's truly just your mind trying its best to take care of you. Once you've learned to recognize the way your mind works, you have the power to retrain it to accept uncertainty. After all, as an adult you now have the life experience and emotional strength needed to deal with tough situations.

Try journaling while worried to understand your fears – what are you imagining? Why? Is there a memory attached?

You could also try a meditative exercise – when you feel worry, take a few deep breaths. Recognize that your thoughts are a result of your brain trying to protect you, thank your mind and then "release" the thought.

EVERYONE STRUGGLES AND IT'S OK TO BE FLAWED BECAUSE THAT'S WHAT MAKES ME, ME.

DEMI LOVATO

KEEP

GOING.

Learn some go-to phrases for anxious moments

Sometimes our anxiety stems from the fear that we are going to say the wrong thing and upset other people and embarrass ourselves. We would be surprised if we realized how rarely people remembered when we misspoke, even when we consider it a mega blooper. If this doesn't help, try having a few humorous scripts ready for when you trip over your words:

- When you make a mistake – Umm, let's try that again.
- When someone hurts your feelings – Ouch!
- When you say something awkward – That came out really weird...

The truth is, everyone feels awkward, out-of-place and embarrassed at times – some are just better at hiding it than others. Acknowledging your own humanness and laughing it off will put you and those around you at ease.

DON'T BELIEVE

everything you think.

Get a morning routine

Let's face it, that first half hour in the morning isn't your best. You're cranky, not fully awake, running on autopilot and it would be really nice if someone could please just do everything for you. So, do yourself a favour and get organized. Prep what you can the night before – that way, "past you" practically does a lot of the morning stuff for "present you". For everything else, get a morning routine – know where you need to be at any given moment between waking up and your morning coffee kicking in and you won't have to worry about forgetting any of it.

YOU MAY NOT CONTROL
ALL THE EVENTS THAT
HAPPEN TO YOU, BUT
YOU CAN DECIDE NOT TO
BE REDUCED BY THEM.

MAYA ANGELOU

LOOK FOR THE GIFTS

You can find positives in absolutely everything, if you look hard enough. An unexpected kindness, a beautiful sunset or an amazing charity shop bargain are all gifts you can't plan for, and it's easy to feel lucky and grateful for these.

On less magical days, you might have to look a bit harder, but rest assured, you'll find a gift! Our hardest days usually hold the most valuable life lessons, ones you can't learn any other way. Even something as sh*tty as a hangover is teaching you about your body's capacity for alcohol and prompting you to rest your body. Thank you, hangover!

LET IT
GO.

TAKE CARE OF SOMETHING OTHER THAN YOURSELF

Being responsible for another living thing doesn't sound super relaxing at first. What if I kill it? What if I make a mess? What if I fail?

Well, what if you... don't?

Taking on a houseplant, vegetable patch or home-brewing project is a great way of showing yourself what you're capable of. Committing to caring for the slow, gentle growth of a natural organism teaches patience. Engaging with nature is linked to greater emotional regulation and decreased anxiety – even small interactions with nature can improve your emotional well-being.

GETTING

help isn't a sign of

WEAKNESS

but a sign of

STRENGTH.

MICHELLE OBAMA

Clean or tidy something

When you're feeling anxious or worried, try tidying a drawer or cleaning your sink. Completing small tasks such as these boosts feelings of well-being, takes your mind off your worries and gives you a sense of accomplishment. On top of that, keeping your environment clean and free from clutter will help you relax, without the constant reminder of chores that the clutter and mess represent.

TALK

TO YOURSELF
LIKE YOU TALK
TO YOUR BFF.

**If it comes, let it come.
If it goes, it's OK, let it go.**

GERMANY KENT

Eat yourself calm

Try to avoid highly processed and high-sugar foods, as these cause your blood sugar levels to peak and crash, taking you on an emotional rollercoaster and wreaking havoc on your anxiety levels.

Instead focus on getting plenty of protein, fresh fruit and veg, wholegrain carbs and staying hydrated. Snacks can be the worst culprits when it comes to anxiety-provoking eating, so swap chocolate and pastries for something healthier such as raw carrots, dates, fresh apple, cashews or plant-based energy bars.

A healthy balanced diet will keep your blood sugar levels even and your hunger in check, keeping you calm and in control.

**SO FAR YOU'VE
SURVIVED 100 PER CENT
OF YOUR WORST DAYS.
YOU'RE DOING GREAT.**

ANONYMOUS

GO FOR A F*CKING WALK

Anxiety and other emotions are controlled in the amygdala – one of the most primitive parts of the human brain. The amygdala's no good at multi-tasking, so if you can get it interested in something else, it will let go of worrying for a while.

Studies have shown that walking can distract the amygdala, effectively quietening the anxious mind while you ramble.

According to science, green spaces are best for mental health, but walking anywhere can help get you out of your head and into the rhythmic movement of your body. Next time you get caught up in anxious thoughts, try a 10-minute stroll round your local area, noticing your surroundings and paying attention to all of your senses.

YOU'VE
GOT

THIS.

F*ck brain chemistry

Worrying often comes from thoughts, but fear and anxiety can pop up just as feelings of unease and distress, meaning sometimes you don't even know what you're worried about, you just feel... worried.

This kind of worry comes from your brain chemistry – your emotions are controlled by the amygdala, while your memories are stored in a part of your brain called the hippocampus. When you have a strong emotional reaction – for example the shock, pain and confusion of being stung by a bee as a child – the event is stored as a long-term memory in the hippocampus. When something triggers this memory in your hippocampus, the amygdala automatically produces the same feelings of fear and distress, even if it's just something that only subconsciously reminded you of that bee sting – like a smell or a song your mind associates with the memory.

When you're feeling overwhelmed, try reminding yourself of this fact.

WHEN YOU GET
TO THE END
OF YOUR ROPE,
TIE A KNOT
AND HANG ON.

ANONYMOUS

STOP TRYING TO CONTROL EVERYTHING

The idea we have a responsibility for how others choose to act can be a huge source of anxiety, especially if we've been blamed for the actions of others in the past.

Here is what you can control: your attitude, actions, effort, words, reactions and expectations.

Here is what you can't control: others' opinions, actions, words and behaviour.

Next time you find yourself worrying, ask yourself if it's within your control. If it is, great! You can do something about it – no need to worry. If it isn't, no need to worry – you can let it go!

Fake it
'til you

MAKE IT.

ARM YOURSELF WITH A CHILL-THE-F*CK-OUT TOOLKIT

As you become more aware of how your worrying mind works, you'll get to know what works for you and what doesn't.

There are a ton of tips in this book, some of which will help you, and some of which won't. When you're stuck in your head, it can be hard to remember what helps. Try keeping a note on your phone, a list in your diary or a reminder on your bedside table to help pull yourself out of a worry-hole.

You might choose one practical tip like going for a walk (page 52), one mental trick like calling out your brain's bullsh*t (page 108) and one lifestyle suggestion like the meditation routine on page 69. Whatever works for you!

WHATEVER THE
PRESENT MOMENT
CONTAINS, ACCEPT
IT AS IF YOU
HAD CHOSEN IT.
ALWAYS WORK
WITH IT, NOT
AGAINST IT.

ECKHART TOLLE

TRACK YOUR MOOD

Try a mood tracker journal or app to notice patterns and trigger points for anxiety. Logging your mood at regular intervals can also help put things in perspective – maybe you spend less time worrying than you thought (yay!). Maybe you spend more time (boo!). Either way, getting a clear idea of how worrying affects you – and having to colour in a little box every time you do it – can help snap you out of the habit.

YOU ARE

[
BOTH A WORK OF ART AND A WORK-IN-PROGRESS.
]

GET BENDY

Gentle stretching-based exercise like yoga or Pilates is a great way to reduce anxiety, give you a sense of calm and help you gain an awareness of your body and emotions. There are plenty of practice options – you can join a regular class, go on a retreat or even find a routine on YouTube. Both disciplines focus on breathing and encourage mindfulness, and there's often a meditation as part of the cool-down part of a class – so you calm your mind and your body!

CONFIDENCE

comes not from always being

RIGHT

but from not fearing to be

WRONG.

PETER T. McINTYRE

Get some perspective

Often, a problem isn't a problem beyond how we think about it and how those thoughts are affecting us emotionally. Try asking yourself some simple questions next time you're driving yourself crazy, you might find it's a lot less of a big deal than it seems:

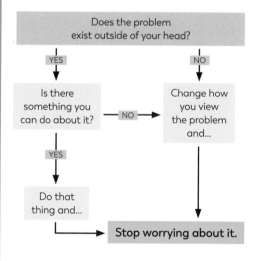

Does the problem exist outside of your head?

YES → Is there something you can do about it?

NO → Change how you view the problem and...

Is there something you can do about it? — NO → Change how you view the problem and...

YES → Do that thing and...

Stop worrying about it.

LET GO

OF WHAT
IFS.

DON'T WORRY
IF YOU'RE NOT
WHERE YOU WANT
TO BE YET. GREAT
THINGS TAKE TIME.

ANONYMOUS

TAKE A F*CKING DAY OFF

The urge to slow down, stay in and wallow around in bed can be strong, especially in the winter months. Taking a duvet day – a day off from work to recuperate when you're not strictly ill – can help calm your worried mind and recharge your batteries. Once you're back to work, duvet days have been found to jump-start motivation and increase productivity.

Try giving yourself permission to forget your responsibilities and spend the day in bed watching trashy TV and eating comfort food. Your body, mind and boss will thank you for it.

I have insecurities of course, but I don't hang out with anyone who points them out to me.

ADELE

MEDITATE

No, really. Don't roll your eyes... close them, sit comfortably and concentrate on your breath.

Notice any sensations in your body. Feel the air flowing in and out of your nostrils.

Picture the spokes of a wheel, with your focus at the centre. If you get distracted, that's your mind sliding down one of the spokes... gently bring it back to the centre. It doesn't matter how many times your mind wanders, what's important is bringing it back to that central focus.

Start by setting a timer for just 3 minutes of meditation every day. As you get used to it, try adding another minute, and so on.

Study after study has found that meditation reduces anxiety and builds mental resilience. Meditation helps by giving you the tools to yank your mind out of an anxious funk and into the moment.

*Give
yourself*

PERMISSION.

F*ck fear

Unless it's an angry bear (in which case drop this book and run) the thing you are scared of doing is probably the exact thing you should be doing.

The human brain likes certainty, comfort and stability, so any kind of change can be perceived as a threat. The mind creates all sorts of thoughts and emotions trying to get you to resist change. That's why even exciting, welcome changes can fill us with fear.

Think of something you're tempted by but fear has stopped you from doing – for example, starting an online business. Take a first step outside your comfort zone by doing one small thing toward it, then another, and another.

Exciting new people, opportunities and experiences reside just outside your comfort zone and you're going to have to tell fear and self-doubt to STFU in order to get to them.

EVERYTHING YOU'VE EVER WANTED IS ON THE OTHER SIDE OF FEAR.

GEORGE ADDAIR

Talk about your f*cking problems

You are allowed to share what's on your mind, you're not a burden. How do you feel when a friend trusts you enough to ask for help? Probably honoured, concerned, eager to help... the other human beings in your life aren't so different to you in this respect.

Be honest with good friends you trust. They'll want to listen and help if they can. Often, just being listened to is the most powerful thing.

WHAT IF

EVERYTHING WORKS OUT FINE?

Go the f*ck outside

It's tempting to stay indoors, especially in the colder months when we want to be wrapped up in cosy blankets.

Even though it can feel good to hide from the world and all its worry-inducing elements, going outside every day, even if it's just for 10 minutes, will help soothe anxiety, lift your mood and improve your physical well-being.

Try getting out into your garden or just walk around the block, even if you don't have any chores that would take you outside. Sunlight, fresh air and gentle exercise – especially if you can get to a park or into the countryside – work wonders on your state of mind and will help ease any worries whirling around in your mind.

JUST BECAUSE I CAN'T
EXPLAIN THE FEELINGS
CAUSING MY ANXIETY
DOESN'T MAKE
THEM LESS VALID.

LAUREN ELIZABETH

GET A HOBBY

Getting lost in a sport, craft or activity that brings you joy will give you a break from real-life stresses and worries. Hobbies foster social connection – a key component to mental well-being – and, depending on the hobby, you can also improve your physical health, master a new skill or nurture your creativity.

If you're stuck for ideas, think back to what fascinated you as a child and see if there's a related hobby you could try. Knitting, historical re-enactment, kickboxing, playing the flute, genealogy... the possibilities are endless.

TRUST

YOUR
GUT.

PRIORITIZE YOUR WELL-BEING

You are the most important person in your life, and you deserve to have your needs met. If that means taking a break from certain responsibilities in order to rest, give yourself permission to put things on the back burner or stop taking on new projects. Having too much on your plate can lead to a constant low-level anxiety. Even if you have others dependent on you, they need you to be healthy and happy in order to be there for them.

NOTHING DIMINISHES ANXIETY FASTER THAN ACTION.

WALTER ANDERSON

Have a good cry

When we're feeling worried or overwhelmed, it's common to start tearing up. Don't resist it! Crying is really beneficial in that it releases emotion, tension and distress trapped in the body. Rather than a sign of weakness, crying is a natural biological function unique to humans, elevating your mood by flooding the brain with feel-good chemical oxytocin. You'll feel better, sleep better and think more clearly after a good cry.

BE PATIENT

*with yourself
– take it one
day, one hour,
one minute,
one breath
at a time.*

KEEP YOUR CIRCLE SMALL

Are there people in your life who make you worry you're not pretty enough, not clever enough, not cool enough?

It's not necessarily their fault – unless they're criticizing and bringing you down – but certain people can trigger feelings of inadequacy in all of us. Gently withdraw from those relationships or establish some boundaries for now. Spend more time with people who make you feel calm, connected and appreciated just as you are.

GOD MADE

the world round

SO WE WOULD

never be able to

SEE TOO FAR

down the road.

KAREN BLIXEN

DO SMALL THINGS

When you're stuck in a worry-hole, things can get blown out of proportion and those tasks you've always taken in your stride suddenly feel impossible. See what feels manageable and give yourself a break about everything else.

Some days it might be completing an assignment or going for a 30-minute run; other days, going to work or college will be enough. Reward yourself with an early night and see what tomorrow brings.

Be gentle with yourself – you're doing fine.

CHILL

[ ]

THE F*CK OUT.

WHO PROFITS FROM THIS EMOTION?

There are several massive industries – fashion, beauty and plastic surgery to name a few – built entirely upon consumers worrying that they are inadequate – that they are in some way either not enough or too much. Next time you find yourself worrying about an aspect of your personality, lifestyle or body, ask yourself this question: "Who profits from this emotion?" (Hint: it's not gonna be you.)

Thinking critically about where your beliefs and anxieties about yourself come from – and whether these messages are worth listening to – will free you from unnecessary worry and pressure.

YOU GAIN
CONFIDENCE BY
DOING THINGS
BEFORE YOU'RE
READY, WHILE
YOU'RE STILL
SCARED.

ELLEN HENDRIKSEN

ASSERT YOUR BOUNDARIES

Boundaries are about owning your responsibilities and letting go of the things you aren't responsible for. Here are some golden rules to help you set and assert your boundaries:

- You can't fix others
- You can say no
- You don't need to be understood or agreed with
- You are allowed to feel what you are feeling
- If it feels wrong, don't do it

Setting boundaries can be intimidating if it's a new concept for you. Trust your own mind and understand that if someone reacts with anger, manipulation or offence to your boundaries, their reaction is their own responsibility, not yours.

F*CKS
GIVEN:
ZERO.

Breathe. That's it. Once more. Good. You're good. Even if you're not, you're alive. You can get better.

N. K. JEMISIN

Know your strengths

Write a long-ass list of everything you're good at, no matter how small or frivolous. Perhaps you make a barn-storming grilled-cheese sandwich or know your way around a sewing machine. Are your limericks the sauciest, your hugs super-snuggly or do you have a great memory for dance routines?

You don't have to be the world champion to be good at something. Write down anything you've succeeded at. Acknowledge, love and cultivate the things you do well, and don't you dare compare them to anyone else's strengths or weaknesses – it's not a competition. Revisit the list whenever you have something new to add, or if you need a confidence boost.

SMILE, BREATHE
AND GO SLOWLY.

THÍCH NHẤT HẠNH

IF YOU'RE NOT FEELING CONFIDENT, JUST FAKE IT

Only a total narcissist would never suffer with self-doubt. Why then, I hear you ask, does everyone else seem so damn confident all the time? The answer: they're either faking it now, or they started out faking it and, at some point, started believing in themselves.

Next time you feel less than Beyoncé-levels of self-confidence, tell yourself you're a badass warrior born to do the thing you're about to do, and act like those words are true (because they are). Before long, you'll see just how capable you really are and faking will become believing.

You can do

ANYTHING

you set your
mind to.

F*ck alcohol

Alcohol can give temporary relief from social anxiety, but the confidence boost you get from three glasses of wine is paid for later when "hanxiety" – the anxiety that accompanies a hangover – strikes.

Alcohol lowers your levels of serotonin – the hormone that brings you feelings of calm and happiness – and the jitteriness and sweating that comes with a hangover can trick your brain into anxiety-mode.

If you're struggling with dips in mood and increased feelings of anxiety after drinking, you may need to adjust how much alcohol you consume. Try alternating alcoholic drinks with a glass of water on a night out, or take some time off from drinking altogether. You could also try socializing in new ways that don't involve booze – going for a walk, coffee or a movie instead of to a bar will help you to avoid the hangover without avoiding your friends.

IT'S OKAY TO
BE CRAZY AND
SCARED AND
BRAVE AT THE
SAME TIME.

KELLY EPPERSON

KEEP A JOURNAL

A journal is like a therapist you keep in your pocket. Pour all your worries, all your tangled or confusing thoughts out of your mind and onto paper. You don't have to find solutions, just the act of expressing them is soothing and recording your worries on paper takes the pressure off your brain from holding onto and processing these thoughts.

Studies have found that regular journaling leads to improved sleep and memory as well as reducing stress, anxiety and depression.

If you've got writer's block, try writing down the things you're worrying about right now. Then, write three things you are looking forward to – big or small. Balancing out negative with positive journaling helps shift your mind into a more resilient and hopeful state.

WHAT WOULD

YOU DO IF YOU KNEW YOU COULD NOT FAIL?

Drink more water

Our bodies rely on having enough water to function properly. Water transports hormones, chemical messages and nutrients to every organ in the body, and when we're lacking water, we can start to feel anxious. Dehydration can have similar effects to a panic attack – racing heart, dizziness, a dry mouth – because your body is desperately trying to get you to drink some f*cking water!

Many of us are in the habit of reaching for sugary or caffeinated drinks throughout the day, which temporarily quench our thirst and give us a boost of energy. But they won't hydrate your body effectively. Drinking plenty of water every day (along with consuming fresh fruit, vegetables, juice and herbal tea) will calm your mind, clear your skin and keep you alert.

THE DOING IS THE THING. THE TALKING AND WORRYING AND THINKING IS NOT THE THING.

AMY POEHLER

ACCEPT YOURSELF AND THE WORLD AS IT IS

Buddhists say the key to inner peace is acceptance. When you stop fighting against reality and focus instead on the present moment, a whole bunch of pointless worrying melts away.

Try accepting your feelings, circumstances and environment exactly as they are at this moment. You don't have to like it, you can still work to change it, but accepting the present moment exactly as it is brings enormous peace by removing the impulse to try to change what we cannot control.

DO YOUR THING.

GO THE F*CK TO SLEEP

Everything seems so much brighter and more manageable after a good night's sleep, but getting to sleep in the first place can be a real pain in the ass when you've got a lot on your mind. Different things work for different people, so here are a few ideas to kick insomnia in the nuts and get more sleep:

- Practise "sleep hygiene" – avoid caffeine, rich food, strenuous exercise and bright lights from electronic devices around bedtime.
- Read a boring book.
- Bring your attention to the top of your head and scan slowly down to your toes.
- If all else fails, know that you are resting your body and that is beneficial in itself, even if you can't drop off.

Insomnia can add to your worries and lead to health problems, so if lack of sleep starts to affect your day-to-day life it's a good idea to see your doctor.

PEACE IS THE RESULT
OF RETRAINING YOUR
MIND TO PROCESS
LIFE AS IT IS, RATHER
THAN AS YOU THINK
IT SHOULD BE.

WAYNE W. DYER

DANCE LIKE NO ONE'S WATCHING

Try living your whole damn life like no one's watching. Here's the white-hot truth: no one is watching... they're focused on themselves, and their own awkward dance moves, just like you are.

Next time you catch yourself holding back from something fun out of fear or self-consciousness, ask yourself: what am I afraid of?

Letting go of the fear of others' judgement is really hard but totally worth it. Wear what you like, love who you love, enjoy yourself and to hell with what anyone else might think.

You are

A WARRIOR,

not a worrier.

*Your brain is a master bullsh*tter*

How much time have you spent worrying about scenarios that never ended up happening? When your brain's getting over-imaginative with its predictions of doom, try asking it: "Is that really likely?"

Asking this question can quickly shine a light on any bullsh*t, stopping worry in its tracks.

Your brain loves inventing the most unlikely, worst-case, one-in-a-bazillion stories, just in case they happen. That's just its way of trying to keep you safe. Er... thanks brain.

Just because you're thinking everyone hates you, or that you're going to epically f*ck up, doesn't make it true or even remotely possible.

SOMETIMES

when you're in a

DARK PLACE

you think you've been

BURIED,

but you've actually been

PLANTED.

CHRISTINE CAINE

LOOK

FEAR IN THE EYE.

THROW YOUR WORRIES INTO THE SEA

Throwing stuff is a truly underrated pastime. It's hella therapeutic and throwing stones into the sea has the added bonus of not hurting anyone or breaking any of your stuff in the process.

Taking a moment to write something you want to let go of onto each stone adds another symbolic level.

Next time you're headed to the beach (or any body of water), take some chalk and write your worries on stones, then chuck them as hard as you can into the sea.

SCREW YOU,

NEGATIVITY.

Recognize your emotions

Excessive worrying can be a way for your brain to distract you from feeling uncomfortable emotions. Because of this it can be hard to put your finger on what you're really feeling when you're worrying.

Try this mindfulness meditation to help recognize and release emotion:

- Sit somewhere quiet and comfortable and close your eyes.
- Take three deep breaths, bringing your attention to your body. What emotion are you feeling? What physical sensations does that emotion bring with it? Does the emotion have a memory or thought attached to it?
- Sit with the emotion. Let it lift you, frighten you or upset you... then let it pass.

Practising this kind of meditation regularly will help you gain control of your thoughts and emotions, leading to a calmer, more peaceful outlook on life.

**If I engage in perfectionism,
I am abusing myself.**

ASHLEY JUDD

ONE STEP AT A TIME

Worrying becomes overwhelming when we see all that needs doing as one huge mountain to be climbed alone. Mindfulness is the tool you use to break that mountain trek into individual steps.

Mindfulness is a discipline. It's the act of drawing your mind into the present moment again and again, away from worry about the future or past.

Next time you have an anxiety-provoking task coming up, like a driving test or work presentation, get strict with your mind.

Tell yourself you are not allowed to think about anything beyond the present moment and the task in hand. No stressing about a mistake you just made, no speculating about what's coming next. Stay rooted in the right now. One step at a time, calm and deliberate until it's done.

Choose

HAPPINESS.

Take a break from your f*cking phone

Seriously. Smartphones take up way too much mental energy. Do not let the glowing rectangle of doom disturb your vibe.

Excessive smartphone usage has been linked to disturbed sleep patterns and increased anxiety, so reducing your phone's capacity to disturb you with notifications and taking control of the urge to check it regularly will help you live your calmest, best life.

IF YOU CAN SOLVE
YOUR PROBLEM,
THEN WHAT IS
THE NEED OF
WORRYING? IF YOU
CANNOT SOLVE IT,
THEN WHAT IS THE
USE OF WORRYING?

SHANTIDEVA

TRUST

[

YOURSELF MORE; YOU'RE DOING GREAT.

]

DO SOME GOOD

Doing stuff for other people feels amazing. Focusing on someone else's needs without the expectation of them reciprocating increases feelings of well-being and gives you a break from your own worries.

Human beings are social creatures, so empathy and altruism are hard-wired into our brains thanks to evolution. Evidence shows that helping others increases happiness levels, bringing with it a sense of belonging, trust and lowered levels of stress and anxiety.

Giving away unwanted items, donating money or volunteering for charity are all excellent ways to give back while boosting your own happiness and self-esteem.

EMBRACE THE UNKNOWN — THAT'S WHERE THE MAGIC IS.

MAKE A DIGITAL HAPPY PLACE

The world can be a scary place. But with apps such as Instagram and Pinterest at your fingertips, it's possible to create a calm little virtual bubble to retreat to in times of anxiety. Ignore the news, perfect celebrity lifestyles and less than appetizing #foodporn by pinning images or following accounts of only things that make you feel happy and relaxed. Cute animal videos, positivity slogans, wholesome memes and satisfying gifs are a great place to start your uplifting mood board.

IF YOU WANT
TO CONQUER THE
ANXIETY OF LIFE,
LIVE IN THE MOMENT,
LIVE IN THE BREATH.

AMIT RAY

Counterintuitive anxiety hacks

When worrying takes hold, it often comes with the urge to act. Try countering worries by doing the opposite of what they are urging you to do.

- If you feel financial pressure → donate some money, possessions or time to a deserving cause
- If you feel alone → meditate
- If you feel time pressure → do something unproductive, like taking a bath
- If you feel unloved → show love to others
- If you feel ugly → take a selfie

Create a little of what you feel you are lacking in the world and watch it come back to you.

Take the

FIRST STEP.

DO TEN JUMPING JACKS

While slowing down and relaxing is super important to becoming less worried in general, sometimes you've got to chase worry away with a bit of vigorous action.

If you feel overwhelmed by worry – perhaps to the point of a panic attack – doing a quick set of jumping jacks gets your attention out of your head and burns off the panicked energy. This will force you to breathe deeply (instead of hyperventilating) and helps reconnect you with the world around you.

THIS FEELING WILL PASS. THE FEAR IS REAL BUT THE DANGER IS NOT.

CAMMIE McGOVERN

BLOW BUBBLES

The deep breathing required to blow bubbles, and even the way you purse your lips when you do it (sounds weird but pursing your lips opens your airways more fully, meaning you'll inhale and exhale more thoroughly, filling your lungs with plenty of fresh oxygen), is excellent for helping you relax. You can even imagine the bubbles are your worries, and you're just blowing them away.

If you feel a little silly, you could blow bubbles in the privacy of your own bathroom.

SLOW

YOUR ROLL.

Hugs not drugs

American therapist Virginia Satir famously recommended four hugs a day for survival, eight for maintenance and twelve for growth.

The jury's out on the optimum number of hugs per day, but research shows that the more you hug, the better you feel. Hugging and being hugged calm your body's stress responses, meaning you're less bothered by outside worries when you're getting regular hugs.

Hugs reduce anxiety in both the hugger and the huggee, and research suggests they boost immunity and lower blood pressure too.

If you're not a natural hugger, try starting the day by offering a hug to someone you're close with like a partner, child or close friend.

I MAY NOT

have gone where I

INTENDED

to go, but I think I have

ENDED UP

where I needed

TO BE.

DOUGLAS ADAMS

Sing along at the top of your voice

Singing – even bad singing... especially bad singing – releases endorphins in the brain, making you feel good (even if you're tone deaf). It opens your airways, increasing oxygen flow to your brain and goddammit, it's fun! Next time you're in need of a pick-me-up, crank up your favourite tune, grab a hairbrush-microphone and belt it out like you're on stage in front of thousands.

YOU CAN NOT BE ALL THINGS

TO ALL PEOPLE.

MAKE A LITTLE STAR

Origami lucky stars are ridiculously cute, obscenely easy and incredibly satisfying to make – check YouTube for simple tutorials. Once you've got your technique sorted, make sure you have a strip of paper handy at all times so you can distract yourself from anxious thoughts by getting absorbed in folding a star.

Having something to do with your hands that's quick but satisfying, simple but beautiful, is a brilliant trick to have up your sleeve for moments of anxiety. Origami has long been employed as a mindfulness practice, with its emphasis on methodical, meditative movements to create beautiful objects. Start with a simple star and get more ambitious if you find it calming – the possibilities are endless.

EACH TIME WE FACE
OUR FEAR, WE GAIN
STRENGTH, COURAGE,
AND CONFIDENCE
IN THE DOING.

THEODORE ROOSEVELT

LET IT GO

Letting go of that job, that person, that opportunity... it's not easy and if you really care, it won't happen overnight. That's why you need to be patient with yourself and keep choosing to let it go every time it comes to mind.

Feel the weight of your disappointment, know that you have created space in your life for new things to come to you, and allow yourself to let go.

Some people find it helps to visualize laying down their grief or worry and letting it float out to sea. Take a few moments to watch it disappear, then see yourself walking away.

LOVE

*yourself
first.*

GET SPIRITUAL

The idea that something bigger than you has your back is incredibly comforting. Some find this in conventional religion, while others look to less structured spiritual belief systems, or invent their own!

We all get to choose what we believe and the meanings we assign to what happens around us. For example, you can choose to write coincidences off as just random occurrences, or you can take them as a hand-squeeze from the universe, letting you know you're on the right track and everything's going to be fine.

**Worry often gives
a small thing
a big shadow.**

SWEDISH PROVERB

START

WHERE YOU ARE.

Take a power nap

Getting plenty of sleep is essential to feeling your best and being mentally robust enough to handle all that life might throw at you. Most of us need 7–9 hours per night for optimal health and longevity, but if your worried mind is keeping you up late or waking you up early, this can be hard to achieve.

Getting enough sleep is really important for regulating your mood, appetite and memory, so if you're not getting enough at night (and you have the opportunity), try taking a "power nap" during the afternoon. A nap lasting 20 minutes is recommended by scientists: any longer and you'll wake up fuzzy-headed, any shorter and you won't reap the mood-enhancing benefits. A lot of people find it difficult to drop off during the day but 20 minutes of resting your eyes and concentrating on your breath will also help you recharge.

GIVE YOUR ATTENTION TO THINGS WHICH FEED YOUR SOUL.

EMBRACE YOUR QUIRKS

We appreciate our friends for their unique qualities, idiosyncrasies and how they make us feel, not for how well they blend in with the rest of the world! It's perfectly possible that the things you find frustrating or annoying about yourself are the things other people love most about you.

So, give yourself a break from worrying about your quirks and recognize them for what they are: the things that make you, you.

RISK ANYTHING!
CARE NO MORE
FOR THE OPINION
OF OTHERS...
DO THE HARDEST
THING ON EARTH
FOR YOU.

KATHERINE MANSFIELD

GROUND YOURSELF

Research shows that connecting with the Earth's natural electrical charge has many mental and physical health benefits, including better sleep, reduced pain and a greater sense of well-being. Try this grounding exercise to connect with your body and the world around you:

* Stand barefoot on grass, sand or soil.
* Close your eyes and let your arms hang by your sides.
* Use your shoulders to swing your arms loosely around your body, repeat five times.
* Now draw your attention to the soles of your feet, noticing the sensation of the ground beneath them.
* Imagine strong roots growing from your feet down into the ground.
* Finish with three deep breaths.

This exercise will help you feel calm, steady and in control – try to get a little barefoot grounding time as often as you can.

NOTHING

is worth sacrificing your mental health for.

HAVE CONFIDENCE
THAT IF YOU HAVE DONE
A LITTLE THING WELL,
YOU CAN DO A BIGGER
THING WELL TOO.

DAVID STOREY

TAKE A F*CKING BUBBLE BATH

Picture the scene: you're sinking into a tub of warm water. There are candles, bubbles glisten invitingly, the smell of lavender fills the room. Worries dissolve in the water like bath salts. Sounds good, right?

Beyond its obvious charms, the humble bubble bath has numerous health benefits too – studies have found that a daily bath boosts circulation, makes you more optimistic and gives you a better night's sleep. They also help synchronize your body's circadian rhythms (which control fluctuations in mood and behaviour throughout the day) leading to decreased stress levels and improved mood.

SOME DAYS YOU'RE THE BUG. SOME DAYS YOU'RE THE WINDSHIELD.

ANONYMOUS

TRY TAROT

No longer the preserve of psychics and side-shows, tarot is gaining in popularity as a tool for self-care. Reading your own tarot cards is less about foretelling the future and more to do with tuning in to your intuition and finding out how you truly feel. Whatever jumps out at you from the imagery of the tarot cards is what your intuition is calling you to pay attention to.

Most tarot decks come with a booklet to help you interpret the cards, but you can just as easily let your gut be your guide. See what you're drawn to in the card, what associations you make between the image and your own life, and what message you're intuiting.

Try bringing your worries or dilemmas to a simple three-card spread to get started:

Past Influence   Current Situation   Future Outcome

YOU ARE

[

AMAZING.

]

DON'T LET

the noise of others'

OPINIONS

drown out your inner

VOICE.

STEVE JOBS

READ A BOOK

Instead of scrolling through your phone, pick up a good book. An absorbing novel will let you escape reality for a while, plus reading has been found to lower your heart rate and increase your self-compassion. Researchers at the University of Sussex have found that just 6 minutes of reading a book can relieve tension in your body by over 60 per cent.

If you're not a big reader, try asking friends for book recommendations, listen to audiobooks, or you could even start your own book club.

BREATHE IN SERENITY,

BREATHE OUT BULLSH*T.

MAKE PROMISES TO YOURSELF – AND KEEP THEM

Trusting in yourself is the key to feeling confident in your abilities and courageous enough to face your fears. When you trust yourself, you know that whatever happens, you will always be OK, because you'll have your own back.

So, how do you build trust? By making and keeping promises. Try promising yourself you'll be in bed by 10 p.m., or that you won't accept invitations to parties you don't want to go to. Start small and manageable, building trust slowly and soon you'll have a solid foundation of self-belief.

WORRY IS A MISUSE OF THE IMAGINATION.

DAN ZADRA

Go to your doctor

While it's true that everyone worries, worrying can get out of hand and morph into something much more challenging. If you're feeling constant or overwhelming anxiety and it's starting to affect your life, health and relationships, it might be time to make an appointment with your doctor.

Asking for help is a sign of strength and self-respect, and you deserve to live your best life, free from excessive worry.

You are

ENOUGH.

F*CK

[

WORRY.

]

If you're interested in finding out more about our books, find us on Facebook at Summersdale Publishers and follow us on Twitter at @Summersdale.

www.summersdale.com

IMAGE CREDITS

pp.10, 41, 50, 75, 92, 108, 130, 160 © Sunward Art/Shutterstock.com

pp.24, 47, 73, 81, 117, 132, 157 © Sunspire/Shutterstock.com

pp.25, 49, 68, 91, 114, 139 © Plasteed/Shutterstock.com